FOOD LOVERS

SOUP

FOOD LOVERS

SOUP

RECIPES SELECTED BY ALEKSANDRA MALYSKA

Trans
Atlantic
Press

All recipes serve four people, unless otherwise indicated.

For best results when cooking the recipes in this book, buy fresh ingredients and follow the instructions carefully. Make sure that everything is properly cooked through before serving, particularly any meat and shellfish, and note that as a general rule vulnerable groups such as the very young, elderly people, pregnant women, convalescents and anyone suffering from an illness should avoid dishes that contain raw or lightly cooked eggs.

For all recipes, quantities are given in standard U.S. cups and imperial measures, followed by the metric equivalent. Follow one set or the other, but not a mixture of both because conversions may not be exact. Standard spoon and cup measurements are level and are based on the following:

1 tsp. = 5 ml, 1 tbsp. = 15 ml, 1 cup = 250 ml / 8 fl oz.

Note that Australian standard tablespoons are 20 ml, so Australian readers should use 3 tsp. in place of 1 tbsp. when measuring small quantities.

The electric oven temperatures in this book are given for conventional ovens with top and bottom heat. When using a fan oven, the temperature should be decreased by about 20–40°F / 10–20°C – check the oven manufacturer's instruction book for further guidance. The cooking times given should be used as an approximate guideline only.

CONTENTS

CHILLED TOMATO SOUP WITH CROUTONS

Ingredients

2¼ lb /1 kg tomatoes

1 onion

3 cloves garlic

1 bunch parsley

1 bunch basil

2 sprigs thyme

1 sprig savory

2 tbsp. olive oil

Salt & freshly milled pepper

2 slices rye bread

3 tbsp. butter, to fry

Method

Prep and cook time: 1 h plus 1 h refrigeration time.

1 Wash, quarter and deseed the tomatoes. Peel and quarter the onion and garlic.

2 Put the tomatoes into a blender with the chopped herbs, onion, garlic and salt and blend.

3 Push through a sieve if you wish. Season to taste with salt and pepper.

4 Stir in the olive oil and chill in the refrigerator for at least an hour.

5 Dice the bread, fry in butter and scatter over the soup before serving.

CREAMY PEA AND LETTUCE SOUP WITH SESAME SEEDS

Ingredients

8 lettuce leaves

2 cups /300 g peas

1 onion

1 tbsp. oil

1¾ cups /400 ml vegetable broth (stock)

2 tbsp. butter

⅓ cup /40 g flour

1¾ cups /400 ml milk

Salt & freshly milled pepper

Pinch nutmeg

¼ cup /50 g whipping cream, whipped

2 tbsp. sesame seeds, toasted

A few sprigs of parsley

Method

Prep and cook time: 35 min

1 Wash and shred the lettuce leaves. Thaw the peas. Peel and finely chop the onion. Heat the oil in a pan and sauté the prepared vegetables. Then add the broth (stock) and simmer for 10–15 minutes.

2 In another pan melt the butter, stir in the flour and cook for a couple of minutes without browning. Gradually stir in the milk and simmer over a low heat for about 5 minutes.

3 Finely purée the pea and lettuce mixture and push through a sieve. Stir into the white sauce and return to a boil. Season with salt and pepper and add nutmeg to taste.

4 Ladle the soup into bowls and add a little whipped cream to each. Sprinkle with toasted sesame seeds, garnish with parsley and serve.

SWEET POTATO SOUP WITH LENTILS AND BALSAMIC ONIONS

Ingredients

1 onion

1 lb 2 oz /450 g sweet potatoes

1 leek

½ cup /100 g red lentils

2 tbsp. /25 g butter

1 clove garlic

1 tsp. ground coriander

4 cups /500 ml vegetable broth (stock)

Salt & freshly milled pepper

2 tbsp. snipped chives

In addition:

2 red onions

1 tbsp. butter

4 tbsp. balsamic vinegar

Balsamic onions, to garnish

Method

Prep and cook time: 1 h

1 Peel and finely dice the onion. Peel and chop the sweet potatoes. Wash, trim and chop the leek. Wash the lentils under running water.

2 Heat the butter and sauté the onion until translucent, press in the garlic and sauté briefly. Stir in the coriander, then add the sweet potatoes and leek and sauté, stirring, for about 5 minutes.

3 Add the vegetable broth (stock) and the lentils, cover and simmer for about 30 minutes.

4 Meanwhile peel and slice the red onions and sauté in butter until soft. Add the balsamic vinegar and simmer until slightly reduced.

5 Remove the soup from the heat, season to taste with salt and pepper, stir in the chives and ladle into plates or bowls. Serve garnished with balsamic onions.

TAMARIND AND COCONUT SOUP

Ingredients

¹/₃ cup /80 ml sesame oil

1 red onion, peeled and chopped

2 cloves garlic, peeled and chopped

1 red chili, chopped

1–2 tsp. cumin

1 tsp. ground coriander

2 very ripe plantains, peeled and cut into ½ inch (1 cm) slices

2½ cups /600 ml chicken broth (stock)

¼ cup /50 ml tamarind paste

1¼ cups /300 ml unsweetened coconut milk

1 tsp. sea salt

½ cup roughly chopped cilantro (coriander) leaves

½ cup roughly chopped fresh mint leaves

Method

Prep and cook time: 30 min

1 Heat the sesame oil in a large pan and add the red onion, garlic, half of the chili, cumin and ground coriander. Sauté for 5 minutes, stirring continuously so it doesn't stick.

2 Add the plantains, broth (stock), tamarind paste and coconut milk and bring to a boil. Turn the heat to a gentle simmer and cook until the plantains are soft, then remove from the heat.

3 Add the salt and purée the soup. Return to the heat and add the rest of the chili.

4 Stir in the cilantro (coriander) and mint just before serving.

SWISS BARLEY SOUP WITH BACON

Ingredients

2 carrots

¾ cup /125 g celery root (celeriac)

2 potatoes

2 leeks

4–5 savoy cabbage leaves

1 onion

1 bay leaf

1 clove

1 tbsp. butter

Scant ½ cup /80 g barley

8 cups /2 litres beef broth (stock)

Salt & freshly milled pepper

4 oz /125 g smoked raw bacon

11 oz /300 g smoked pork

7 oz /200 g smoked beef

Strips of savoy cabbage, to garnish

Method

Prep and cook time: 2 h 20 min

1 Peel the carrots, celery root (celeriac) and potatoes and finely chop. Wash and trim the savoy cabbage leaves and finely slice. Peel the onion and push the clove and bay leaf into the onion.

2 Heat the butter in a large sauce pot. Fry the vegetables in the butter, add the barley and sauté.

3 Pour in the beef broth (stock) and season with salt and pepper. Add the onion, bacon, pork and beef, cover and simmer for about 2 hours.

4 Take the meat, bacon and onion out of the pot and cut into bite-size pieces. Put in the soup.

5 Season to taste and serve garnished with strips of savoy cabbage.

SPICY CHESTNUT SOUP

Ingredients

1 clove garlic

1 red onion

7 oz /200 g tomatoes

2 tbsp. olive oil

¾–1 cup /200 ml red wine

2½ cup /600 ml vegetable broth (stock)

3½ oz /100 g chestnut purée, canned

¼ cup /50 ml cream whipping cream

1 sprig rosemary

2 oz /60 g bacon

2 tbsp. balsamic vinegar

1 tbsp. tomato purée

1 tbsp sugar

7 oz /200 g porcini

Salt & freshly milled pepper

Method

Prep and cook time: 40 min

1 Peel and finely chop the onion and garlic. Finely dice the chestnuts. Drop the tomatoes into boiling water for a few seconds, refresh in cold water, peel, deseed and finely chop the flesh.

2 Heat the olive oil in a pan and sauté the garlic and onion until translucent. Stir in ²/₃ cup (150 ml) red wine. Add the chestnuts, tomatoes, chestnut purée, cream, vegetable broth (stock) and rosemary and simmer over a low heat for about 15 minutes.

3 Finely dice the bacon and fry until crisp. Add the rest of the red wine and simmer for 5 minutes with the balsamic vinegar, tomato purée and sugar. Clean and finely chop the porcini, add to the pan and fry briefly.

4 Season the soup with salt and pepper, ladle into plates and garnish with the mushroom mixture.

CREAMED PUMPKIN SOUP WITH GINGER AND STRIPS OF CHILI

Ingredients

1 lb /500 g pumpkin, diced

1 onion

1 clove garlic

1 tsp. fresh ginger, chopped

2 tbsp. butter

3¼ cups /800 ml vegetable broth (stock)

¾–1 cup /200 ml light (single) cream

2 tbsp chopped walnuts

Salt

Cayenne pepper

Brown sugar

Chili threads, dried

Method

Prep and cook time: 45 min

1 Peel the pumpkin, remove the seeds and dice. Peel the onion and the garlic and finely chop.

2 Sauté the pumpkin, onion, garlic and ginger in hot butter, then pour in the vegetable broth (stock) and cream. Simmer over a low heat for about 30 minutes.

3 In the meantime roughly chop the walnuts and toast in a dry, hot skillet.

4 Purée the soup, season with salt, cayenne pepper and sugar and spoon into 4 bowls. Garnish with the chopped walnuts and chili threads and serve.

BOUILLON NIPPON WITH DUCK BREAST

Ingredients

1 duck breast fillet
(about 10 oz /300 g)

Salt & freshly milled pepper

6¼ cups /1½ litres strong chicken broth (stock)

1 inch /3 cm piece fresh ginger

1 chili

1 large carrot

2 scallions (spring onions)

2 oz /50 g narrow ribbon noodles

2½ oz /60 g small bean sprouts (soybean or mung bean)

3½ oz /100 g slice tofu

1 hard-boiled egg

Soy sauce

Method

Prep and cook time: 1 h

1 Score the skin of the duck breast in a diamond pattern and season with salt and pepper. Then lay in a cold skillet, skin side down, and heat. Turn over as soon as the fat runs. Fry for about 7 minutes, then turn and fry for about a further 7 minutes until crisp. Take out and set aside.

2 Peel and slice the ginger. Wash and deseed the chili. Put the ginger and chili into the broth (stock), cover and simmer for 15 minutes. Strain the broth through a sieve.

3 Peel and wash the carrot and cut into thin strips lengthways (or into shapes using a cutter). Wash and trim the scallions (spring onions) and cut into rings at an angle.

4 Cook the noodles according to the package instructions, drain and refresh in cold water.

5 Rinse the bean sprouts in cold water and drain. Dice the tofu. Shell and slice the egg. Cut the duck breast into thin slices.

6 Divide the noodles, vegetables, tofu, egg and meat between soup bowls, add hot broth and season to taste with soy sauce. Serve at once.

COLD BORSCHT

Ingredients

1 lb 8 oz /750 g beet (beetroot)

1 onion

1 clove garlic

3½ oz /100 g white cabbage

3½ oz /100 g leek

2 tbsp. butter

3 cups /750 ml vegetable broth (stock)

1–2 tbsp. white wine vinegar

Good ½ cup /200 g sour cream

Salt & freshly milled pepper

4 hard-boiled quails' eggs (or small hens' eggs)

Dill weed (tips) to garnish

Method

Prep and cook time: 30 min, plus 1 hour refrigeration time

1 Thinly peel and grate the beet (beetroot). Peel and finely chop the onion and garlic. Shred the cabbage. Wash the leek and cut into rings.

2 Heat the butter in a pan and sauté the onion and garlic. Add the cabbage, leek and beet and sauté briefly. Add the vegetable broth (stock), bring to a boil and simmer over a low heat for about 20 minutes.

3 Then purée the soup, stir in the sour cream and season to taste with vinegar, salt and pepper. Chill until time to serve.

4 To serve, shell and halve the eggs. Ladle the soup into bowls or plates, place 2 egg halves in the middle of each and garnish with dill weed.

MUSSEL SOUP WITH PASTIS AND TARRAGON

Ingredients

1 lb 12 oz /800 g fresh mussels

1 small fennel bulb

3½ cups /800 ml water

1 cup /250 ml white wine

2 bay leaves

Salt & freshly milled pepper

1 cup /250 ml whipping cream

3 tbsp. Pastis liquor

½ tsp. mustard

Tarragon

Method

Prep and cook time: 35 min

1 Wash the mussels well in cold water, debeard and let drain. Discard any mussels that are open.

2 Wash, trim and halve the fennel, remove the stalk and chop the rest of the bulb. Put the water into a pan with the wine, bay leaves and salt and bring to a boil.

3 Add the mussels, return to a boil and after about 3 minutes take out again with a skimmer; discard any mussels that have not opened.

4 Put the fennel into the stock and simmer for about 10 minutes. Add the cream to the stock and return to a boil.

5 Add the pastis, mustard and pepper and check the seasoning. Return the mussels to the soup, reheat and serve garnished with tarragon.

CHICKEN SOUP WITH CUCUMBER, SPROUTS AND MINT

Ingredients

2 tbsp. oil

2 chicken breast fillets, cut into strips

2 tsp. yellow curry paste

3 cloves garlic, peeled and chopped

2 tsp. freshly grated ginger root

1 tsp. ground coriander

1 tsp. turmeric

1 tsp. sugar

½ tsp. grated lemon zest

3–4 tbsp. lemon juice

1 tbsp. fish sauce

3 shallots, thinly sliced

4 cups /1 litre chicken broth (stock)

1¾ cups /400 ml coconut milk, unsweetened

7 oz /200 g fresh Chinese egg noodles

1 cup /100 g bean sprouts

3 shallots, thinly sliced

Cucumber slices and mint leaves, to garnish

Method
Prep and cook time: 30 min

1 Heat the oil in a large pan. Sauté the chicken, stirring, for about 4 minutes. Add the curry paste, garlic, ginger, coriander, turmeric, sugar and lemon zest and cook for 3–4 minutes, stirring constantly.

2 Add the lemon juice, fish sauce, sliced shallots, chicken broth (stock) and coconut milk, bring to a boil and simmer, uncovered, for about 15 minutes.

3 Meanwhile cook the noodles in a pan of water for 5–7 minutes, or until soft, drain through a sieve.

4 Put the noodles in bowls and fill up with soup. Garnish with bean sprouts, cucumber slices and mint leaves and serve immediately.

NOODLE SOUP WITH ASPARAGUS

Ingredients

14 oz /400 g lean stewing beef

1 onion

1 carrot

1 leek

1 stick celery

½ bunch parsley

Salt & freshly milled pepper

1 piece ginger (2 inches /5 cm)

2 tbsp. sesame oil

For the noodle soup:

11 oz /300 g Chinese egg noodles

9 oz /250 g fresh green asparagus

1 piece fresh ginger (1 inch /3 cm)

Wasabi

2 slices smoked salmon, cut into strips

Method
Prep and cook time: 1 h 20 min

1 Wash the soup vegetables and prepare as appropriate, then chop roughly. Slice the ginger. Put the meat into a large pan with the soup vegetables and add sufficient water just to cover. Add the parsley, ginger, salt and pepper, cover and bring to a boil. Reduce the heat and simmer over a low heat for about 60 minutes.

2 Strain through a fine sieve and catch the broth in a second pan. Take out the meat and use for another dish.

3 Wash the asparagus and cut off the woody ends. Blanch in plenty of salted water for about 8 minutes, then drain. Cut the ginger into wafer thin slices.

4 Cook the noodles according to the package instructions and drain.

5 Reheat the broth and season with salt and pepper. Stir in the sesame oil. Then add the asparagus and sliced ginger. Leave to infuse for a while (do not let it boil again), then ladle into small bowls and serve with wasabi and strips of smoked salmon.

THAI CHICKEN SOUP WITH COCONUT MILK

Ingredients

14 oz /about 400 g chicken breast

1 cup /100 g oyster mushrooms

2 medium sized tomatoes

1 red chili

1¾ cups /400 ml coconut milk, can, unsweetened

2¼ cups /600 ml water

1–2 tsp. ginger, freshly grated

4 tbsp. fish sauce

4 tbsp. lime juice

Sugar

Salt

1 tbsp. freshly copped cilantro (coriander)

Method

Prep and cook time: 35 min

1 Cut the chicken breasts into bite-size pieces. Clean the oyster mushrooms and slice. Wash, quarter, de-seed the tomatoes and chop. Wash the chili, cut in half lengthways, de-seed and finely chop.

2 Heat the coconut milk in a pan together with the water and bring to a boil.

3 Add the chicken, mushrooms, tomatoes, ginger and chili and season to taste with fish sauce and lime juice. Simmer for about 5 minutes. Add sugar and salt to taste and sprinkle chopped cilantro (coriander) over the top and serve.

LENTIL SOUP
WITH SAUSAGE AND LEEKS

Ingredients

¾ cup /150 g brown lentils

2 carrots

10 oz /300 g potatoes, boiling

1 leek

1 tbsp. oil

4 oz /100 g bacon cubes

1 onion, chopped

1 clove garlic, finely chopped

2 cloves

1 bay leaf

6 cups /1½ litres beef broth (stock)

10 oz /300 g Bologna, Lyoner or Mortadella sausage, cut into rings

Salt & freshly milled pepper

2 tbsp. chopped fresh parsley, to garnish

Method

Prep and cook time: 1 h Soaking time: 12 h

1 Rinse the lentils under cold water in a sieve. Place in a bowl, cover with fresh water and soak overnight. Drain well.

2 Peel and dice the carrots and the potatoes. Wash and trim the leek and cut into 2 inch (5 cm) long, thin strips. Heat the oil in a large pan and sauté the bacon, onions and garlic until soft. Add the carrots, potato and leek and sauté. Now throw in the bay leaf and the cloves, pour in the beef broth (stock) and add the lentils. Bring to a boil, then reduce the heat and simmer for about 45 minutes. Remove the bay leaf and the cloves. Process about one third of the soup in a blender until smooth. Pour back into the soup.

3 Peel the skin off the sausage and cut into thin rings. Place in the soup and simmer for 5 minutes. Season with salt and pepper. Serve in bowls and garnish with the chopped parsley.

GARLIC SOUP WITH BREAD

Ingredients

12 cloves garlic

1 sprig sage

4¼ cups /1 litre vegetable broth (stock)

2 tbsp. olive oil

2 bay leaves

1 cup /100 g grated Parmesan cheese

2 egg yolks

2 tbsp. whipping cream

Salt & freshly milled pepper

2 tbsp. sherry

1 tbsp. lemon juice

1 tbsp. mustard

4 toasted baguette slices

Fresh parsley, to garnish

Method
Prep and cook time: 30 min

1 Peel the garlic and wash the sage leaves. Put into a pan with the vegetable broth (stock), bay leaves and olive oil and bring to a boil. Simmer, half-covered with a lid, for 15 minutes.

2 Take out the bay leaves and sage and purée the soup with a hand blender.

3 Mix the Parmesan cheese, egg yolks and cream.

4 Remove the soup from the heat and carefully stir in the cheese mixture. Season with salt and pepper and add sherry, lemon juice and mustard to taste.

5 Ladle the soup into 4 soup bowls and add a toasted baguette slice to each. Serve garnished with garlic and the parsley.

FISH SOUP WITH POTATOES

Ingredients

2 tbsp. olive oil

2 onions, finely chopped

2 cloves garlic, finely chopped

1–2 small red chilies, de-seeded and finely chopped

1 packet saffron threads

14 oz /400 g chopped canned tomatoes

1 tbsp. tomato paste (purée)

¾–1 cup /200 ml white wine

14 oz /400 g small whole potatoes, for boiling

Salt & freshly milled pepper

12 oz /350 g mixed seafood, such as mussels, clams, shrimps, squid

1 lb 6 oz /600 g fish fillets, such as cod, perch, tuna

½ bunch fresh parsley, chopped

Method

Prep and cook time: 1 h

1 Heat the olive oil in a large skillet. Fry the onions, garlic, chili and saffron threads over a medium heat for about 10 minutes.

2 Add the tomatoes, tomato paste (purée) and pour in the white wine. Bring to a boil, then reduce the heat and simmer for 5 minutes.

3 Peel the potatoes and dice if necessary, and then add to the pan and simmer gently for 15 minutes. Season with salt and pepper.

4 Wash and clean the seafood and add to the soup. Place the fish fillets on the top. Cover and simmer for a further 10 minutes over a medium heat.

5 Spoon into 4 bowls, sprinkle with freshly chopped parsley and serve.

FRENCH ONION SOUP WITH CHEESE BAGUETTES

Ingredients

For the soup:

2¼ lbs /1 kg onions

2 oz /50 g butter

4 cups /1 litre vegetable broth (stock)

1 cup /240 ml dry red wine

Pinch nutmeg

1 tsp. fresh or ½ tsp. dried thyme

Pinch ground caraway

Salt & freshly milled pepper

For the garnish:

4–8 slices baguette

2 cloves garlic, peeled

2 oz /50 g Gruyere cheese, grated

Bunch fresh parsley, finely chopped

Method

Prep and cook time: 45 min

1 Peel the onions and finely slice. Heat the butter in a large pan and fry the onions until soft. Pour in the vegetable broth (stock) and the wine and season with nutmeg, thyme and ground caraway. Bring to a boil, and then simmer for 25–30 minutes.

2 Toast the slices of baguette and rub a peeled garlic clove over the top of the baguette, then use a garlic press to crush the rest of the garlic into the soup.

3 Season the soup with salt and pepper and spoon into 4 ovenproof bowls. Arrange the baguette slices on top of the soup, sprinkle the grated cheese over the top and grill for a few minutes until the cheese has melted.

4 Sprinkle with finely chopped parsley and serve.

KALE AND SPINACH SOUP

Ingredients

10 oz /300 g kale, shredded

4 oz /100 g spinach, shredded

4 oz /100 g kohlrabi, sliced (or turnip if not available)

3 oz /75 g carrots, diced

7 oz /200 g baking potatoes, diced

1 clove garlic

1 onion

1½ oz /40 g smoked bacon

2 tbsp. oil

Scant ½ cup /100 ml white wine

3¼ cups /800 ml vegetable broth (stock)

1 tsp. lemon juice

Salt & freshly milled pepper

For the garnish:

4 oz /100 g white sandwich bread, diced

1 oz /25 g butter

2 tbsp. crème fraîche

Grated Parmesan cheese, to garnish

Method

Prep and cook time: 50 min

1 Wash and trim the spinach and the kale and finely shred. Peel the kohlrabi, carrots, potatoes, garlic and onion. Thinly slice the kohlrabi and dice the carrots and the potatoes.

2 Finely chop the onion, garlic and the bacon.

3 Heat the oil in a large pan and sauté the onions, garlic and bacon, stirring continually. Add the kale, spinach and kohlrabi and sauté, and then pour in the white wine and the vegetable broth (stock). Bring to a boil, and then simmer over a low heat for about 20 minutes.

4 Take about ⅓ of the vegetables out of the pot and put on the side. Finely purée the soup and season to taste with salt, pepper and lemon juice. Put the vegetables back into the soup and warm.

5 Cut the crusts off the white sandwich bread and cut into small cubes. Melt the butter in a skillet and toss the croutons in the butter until golden brown. Take out of the skillet and season with salt. Spoon the soup into 4 soup bowls, put a few croutons over the top, a spoonful of crème fraîche and serve with a sprinkle of grated Parmesan cheese.

MEDITERRANEAN VEGETABLE STEW WITH FISH DUMPLINGS

Ingredients

1 red bell pepper

1 yellow bell pepper

5 oz /150 g fennel

4 oz /120 g carrots

3½ oz /100 g celery

1 red onion

3½ oz /100 g zucchini (courgettes)

½ cup /80 g peas, fresh or frozen

10 cherry tomatoes

1 red chili

1 clove garlic

2 tbsp. olive oil

2 tbsp. finely chopped herbs (parsley, chives, tarragon)

about 4-6 cups /1–1^1/5 liters fish broth (stock)

Salt & freshly milled pepper

For the fish dumplings:

9 oz /250 g cod (without skin or bones

½-¾ cups /150–200 ml cream

1 egg white

1½ tbsp. sherry

½ tsp. lemon juice

A dash of Tabasco sauce

Ingredients for the dumpling cooking liquid:

Salted water

2 sprigs thyme

White wine vinegar

Method

Prep and cook time: 1 h

1 Quarter and core the bell peppers. Trim the fennel and celery. Peel the carrots and onions. Cut the ends off the zucchini (courgettes). Cut all the vegetables into approximately 1½ inch (4 cm) strips.

2 Halve the tomatoes. Set aside. Remove the stalk from the chili and cut the chili into rings, removing the seeds in the process. Peel and slice the garlic and fry in olive oil.

3 Put all the vegetables (except the peas, zucchini and tomatoes) into a large pan with the broth (stock) and cook until soft. Add the peas and zucchini 5 minutes, and the tomatoes and chili 2 minutes before the end of cooking time. Add the garlic and the oil it was fried in and season with salt, pepper and herbs.

4 For the dumplings, dice the fish and chop roughly in a food processor. Chill the cream and fish separately in the freezing compartment, then purée the fish, at the same time gradually adding the ice-cold cream and the egg white, to produce a glossy, compact mixture. This must then be pushed through a fine sieve. It is important to stand the bowl containing the dumpling mixture in a bowl of cold water throughout. Season to taste with lemon juice, Tabasco and sherry.

5 Shape into dumplings using two spoons and cook very gently in the cooking liquid for 10-12 minutes.

6 Ladle the stew onto plates and add the fish dumplings.

GREEN BEAN SOUP WITH CREAM

Ingredients

14 oz /400 g green beans, blanched

1–2 potatoes

1 small onion

1 stick celery

1–2 carrots

½ leek

2 tbsp. oil

3¼ cups /800 ml vegetable broth (stock)

1 tbsp. savory

Salt & freshly milled pepper

2 tbsp. chopped parsley

1 tsp. chopped rosemary

Scant ½ cup /100 ml whipping cream

Method

Prep and cook time: 45 min

1 Wash the beans and cut into approximately 1 inche (3 cm) lengths. Peel and dice the potatoes, onion, celery and carrots. Wash, trim and quarter the leek and cut into small pieces.

2 Heat the oil in a pan and sauté all the vegetables. Then add the broth (stock) and the savory and simmer for 20–30 minutes. Season with salt and pepper, add herbs and cream to taste and serve.

GREEN POTATO SOUP

Ingredients

1 lb 2 oz /500 g potatoes

2 cloves garlic

2 scallions (spring onions)

1 bunch celery root (celeriac) leaves
(or buy 1 celery root with leaves)

Salt & freshly milled pepper

Nutmeg

4 cups /1 litre vegetable broth (stock)

4 tbsp. crème fraîche

2 tbsp. whipping cream

2 slices bacon

Method

Prep and cook time: 45 min

1 Peel and dice the potatoes. Wash the celery root (celeriac) leaves; reserve a few to garnish and shred the rest. Wash and trim the scallions (spring onions) and cut into rings.

2 Put the scallions into a pan with the potatoes, celery leaves and vegetable broth (stock). Press the garlic into the pan and bring to a boil. Season well with salt, pepper and nutmeg. Simmer gently for 25 minutes, then purée with a hand blender.

3 Cut the bacon rashers in half and fry in a skillet until crisp.

4 Stir the cream and crème fraîche into the soup, check the seasoning and ladle into four bowls.

5 Lay a piece of bacon on top of each and scatter with celery root leaves.

HERB SOUP WITH CROÛTONS

Ingredients

4 oz /100 g spinach

1–2 handfuls mixed herbs (chervil, parsley, basil, sorrel)

1–2 shallot

4 oz /100 g potatoes

2 tbsp. butter

3 cups /700 ml chicken broth (stock)

Scant ½ cup /100 g whipping cream)

2 tbsp. crème fraîche

Salt & freshly milled pepper

To garnish:

2 slices white bread

2 tbsp. butter

Bunch fresh parsley

Method
Prep and cook time: 40 min

1 Wash the spinach and blanch in boiling, salted water for a few minutes. Refresh in cold water, drain well, and then chop.

2 Wash the herbs and shake dry. Peel and finely chop the shallots. Peel and finely grate the potatoes.

3 Sauté the shallots in hot butter until soft. Pour in the chicken broth (stock) and add the potatoes. Simmer for about 10 minutes. Now pour in the cream, crème fraîche, spinach and the herbs. Bring to a boil, then purée until smooth.

4 Cut the crusts off the bread and cut into cubes. Fry in hot butter until golden brown.

5 Season the soup to taste with salt and pepper and serve with a few croutons and a few sprigs of parsley.

RED LENTIL SOUP

Ingredients

1 lb /450g pack of soup vegetables; carrot, celery root (celeriac), leek

2 cups /400 g red lentils

4 cups / 1 litre beef broth (stock)

1 bay leaf

1 tsp. dried thyme

2 tsp. lemon zest, grated

1 tbsp. tomato concentrate

3 tbsp. balsamic vinegar

Salt & freshly milled pepper

Pinch sugar

For the garnish:

2 slices wholemeal bread

2 tbsp. butter

Fresh basil leaves, shredded

Method

Prep and cook time: 40 min

1 Wash the soup vegetables and peel the carrot and celery root (celeriac). Finely chop. Wash the lentils in a sieve under cold, running water, then place in the beef broth (stock) and bring to a boil.

2 Add the chopped vegetables, the bay leaf and the thyme and simmer for about 20 minutes. As soon as the lentils are soft, remove the bay leaf and purée the soup.

3 Cut the crusts off the bread, cut the bread into cubes and fry in the butter until golden brown. Set aside.

4 Put the grated lemon zest and tomato concentrate in the soup, cover with a lid and warm through. Season with balsamic vinegar, salt, pepper and a pinch of sugar. Serve in warmed bowls, sprinkle a few croutons over the top and garnish with shredded basil leaves.

BROCCOLI SOUP WITH CORN KERNELS AND MUSHROOMS

Ingredients

1 onion

3 cloves garlic

1 head of broccoli

7 oz /200 g button mushrooms

10 oz /280 g can of corn kernels

3 tbsp. butter

3¼ cups / 800 ml vegetable broth (stock)

1 tbsp. flour

Scant ½ cup / 100 g whipping cream

Salt & freshly milled pepper

1 tbsp. finely chopped parsley leaves

Method

Prep and cook time: 40 min

1 Peel and finely chop the onion and garlic. Wash the broccoli and divide into small florets. Clean the mushrooms and cut into smaller pieces if necessary. Drain the corn kernels.

2 Heat 2 tablespoons of the butter in a pan and sauté the onion and garlic until translucent. Add the mushrooms and broccoli and sauté all together. Add the broth (stock) and bring to a boil. Reduce the heat, cover and simmer for 15 minutes.

3 Blend together the remaining butter and the flour and stir the paste into the soup. Stir in the cream and corn kernels and briefly bring to a boil.

4 Season with salt and pepper

SCALLOP CHOWDER

Ingredients

Butter, to fry

1 large white onion, finely chopped

2 red bell peppers

1 leek, sliced

4 cups /1 litre clear fish or vegetable broth (stock)

3 small, tart apples, cored and cut into wedges

Scant–1 cup /200 g light (single) cream

4 tbsp. thyme leaves

Salt & freshly milled pepper

20 fresh scallops

4 sprigs fresh thyme

Method

Prep and cook time: 40 min

1 Gently heat the butter in a pan and sauté the onion until translucent. Add the bell peppers and leek and sauté all together for a few minutes. Add the fish broth (stock) and bring to a boil. Reduce the heat and simmer the soup over a low heat for 10 minutes.

2 Add the apple wedges and cook for 5 more minutes. Add the cream and thyme leaves and season to taste with salt and pepper. Simmer for a further 2–3 minutes, then add the scallops to the soup. Heat for 3–4 minutes until the scallops are cooked.

3 Garnish the soup with fresh thyme and serve. Toasted white bread or garlic bread goes well with this dish.

CREAMY BLUE CHEESE SOUP

Ingredients

1 onion

1 lb 2 oz /500 g celery root (celeriac)

8 tbsp. olive oil

3¼ cups /800 ml chicken or vegetable broth (stock)

2 thin slices white bread

3 oz /80 g Roquefort cheese

¾–1 cup /200 g whipping cream

Salt & freshly milled pepper

Nutmeg

Celery root (celeriac) leaves, to garnish

2 tsp. sour cream to garnish

Method

Prep and cook time: 40 min

1 Peel and finely dice the onion. Wash, peel and roughly dice the celery root (celeriac).

2 Heat 3 tbsp olive oil in a pan and sauté the onion and celery root for 1 minute. Add the hot chicken broth (stock) and cook over a medium heat for 10 minutes.

3 Cut the crusts off the bread, roughly dice the bread and add to the soup. Cook for a further 10 minutes.

4 Stir in the crumbled cheese and let the soup cool slightly then purée finely. Stir in the cream and reheat, and then season to taste with salt, pepper and nutmeg.

5 Ladle the soup into four soup plates and serve garnished with celery root leaves and sour cream.

SPICY CORN CREAM SOUP WITH FRIED BACON

Ingredients

10 oz /280 g can of corn kernels

1 onion, diced

2½ cups / 600 ml vegetable broth (stock)

1 small chili, finely diced

Salt & freshly milled pepper

Chili powder

Sugar

1½ tbsp. butter

3 tbsp. flour

Scant ½ cup / 100 g whipping cream

2 oz /50 g bacon, thinly sliced

Parsley, to garnish

Method

Prep and cook time: 30 min

1 Drain the corn kernels. Put about ¾ of the can into a small pan and add the onion, broth (stock), ¾ of the chili and seasonings and simmer, stirring occasionally, for 10–15 minutes.

2 Blend together the butter and flour to make a paste and stir it into the broth. Briefly bring the soup to a boil.

3 Finely purée the soup, adding the cream at the same time (push through a sieve if you wish). Add the rest of the sweetcorn into the soup.

4 Fry the diced bacon in a dry skillet until crisp.

5 Reheat the soup and serve sprinkled with the bacon, parsley and the rest of the chili.

SHRIMP AND NOODLE SOUP (LAKSA)

Ingredients

For the curry paste:

1 shallot

2 cloves garlic

1 in (3 cm) piece of fresh ginger,

1–2 stalks lemon grass

1 tbsp. fish sauce

1 tbsp. sambal oelek or other chili sauce

1–2 tbsp. lime juice

1 tsp. cumin

For the soup:

1 bunch cilantro (coriander)

3–4 scallions (spring onions)

8 oz /250 g bean sprouts

5 oz /150 g tofu

1–2 tbsp. oil

3 cups /700 ml fish broth (stock)

1 tsp. shrimp paste

1¹⁄₃ cups/350 ml coconut milk

14 oz /400 g shrimps (or prawns) cleaned and prepared

3½ oz / 100 g glass noodles

Method

Prep and cook time: 1 h

1 For the curry paste, peel the shallot and garlic and chop both very finely. Peel the ginger and grate very finely. Trim the lemon grass and chop very finely. Mix the shallot, garlic, ginger and lemon grass and purée finely with the rest of the ingredients.

2 Wash the coriander (cilantro) and pick the leaves off the stem and chop the leaves. Trim the scallions (spring onions) and cut into thin rings. Wash and drain the bean sprouts. Dice the tofu.

3 Heat the oil in a skillet and sauté the tofu until golden brown. Take out of the skillet and set aside. Mix the fish broth (stock) with the shrimp and curry pastes. Put into a saucepan and bring to a boil then reduce the heat and add the coconut milk, shrimps, scallions and tofu. Simmer gently for 2 minutes. Then add the bean sprouts and simmer for a further 1–2 minutes.

4 Stir in the cilantro, reserving a little for garnish. Cook the glass noodles according to instructions on the packet.

5 Drain the noodles and divide between 4 soup bowls while still hot. Ladle the soup over the noodles and serve garnished with cilantro.

CREAMED LEEK AND PEA SOUP

Ingredients

2 leeks

1 clove garlic

1 lettuce

2 oz /50 g butter

1 tsp. chopped thyme leaves

4 cups / 1 litre chicken or vegetable broth (stock)

1¾ cups /280 g frozen peas

1 tbsp. chopped mint leaves

1⅓ cups /300 g whipping cream

Salt & freshly milled pepper

Croutons, to garnish

Method

Prep and cook time: 25 min

1 Wash and trim the leeks and cut into rings. Peel and chop the garlic. Wash and shred the lettuce.

2 Heat the butter in a pan and sauté the leeks, thyme and garlic. Add the broth (stock) and bring back to a boil. Add the peas and lettuce and simmer gently for 5–6 minutes, until the peas are soft.

3 Remove from the heat and purée finely. Add the mint and cream and return to a boil. Season with salt and pepper and serve scattered with croutons

LAMB AND CABBAGE SOUP

Ingredients

14 oz / 400 g lamb, from the leg

2 potatoes, boiling

½ small white cabbage

1 carrot

1 cup /200 g pumpkin, or squash

1 onion

2 cloves garlic

2 tbsp. olive oil

5 oz /150 g bacon, diced

4 cups /1 litre lamb broth (stock)

7 oz /200 g cauliflower florets

1 tsp. grated ginger

Salt & freshly milled pepper

Good pinch of chili powder

2 tbsp. chopped fresh dill

Method

Prep and cook time: 55 min

1 Roughly dice the lamb. Peel the potatoes and cut into cubes. Wash and shred the cabbage. Peel and slice the carrot. Peel and dice the pumpkin or squash. Peel and finely chop the onion and garlic.

2 Heat the oil in a casserole dish and brown the meat on all sides over a medium heat. Add the bacon, onion and garlic and fry all together briefly. Stir in the broth (stock) and add all the other vegetables. Cover and simmer over a low heat for about 45 minutes.

3 Season with salt, pepper and chilli powder. Sprinkle fresh dill over the top before serving.

HOT AND SOUR SHRIMP SOUP

Ingredients

4 oz /125 g straw mushrooms, enoki or white mushrooms

1 stalk lemon grass

5 hot green Thai chilies

3 cups /700 ml chicken broth (stock)

2 cloves garlic, chopped

3 kaffir lime leaves

2 slices fresh galangal, if available

1–2 tbsp. fish sauce

7 oz /200 g shrimps (or prawns), cleaned and shelled

1–2 tbsp. lime juice

A few cilantro (coriander) leaves, to garnish

Method

Prep and cook time: 20 min

1 Clean and slice the mushrooms. Cut the lemon grass stalk into about 1 in (3 cm) lengths. Wash the chilies and slice diagonally.

2 Pour the chicken broth (stock) into a saucepan and bring to a boil, then reduce the heat. Add the garlic, lemon grass, mushrooms, chilies, lime leaves, galangal and 1 tablespoon of fish sauce and simmer for about 4 minutes. Add the shrimps and cook very gently for about 1 minute.

3 Remove the lemon grass from the soup. Season to taste with fish sauce and lime juice and serve garnished with cilantro (coriander) leaves.

CORN CREAM SOUP WITH DICED POLENTA

Ingredients

For the polenta cubes:

½–⅔ cup / 100 g cornmeal, or instant polenta

2 cups / 500 ml water

½ tsp. salt

2 tbsp. butter

2 tbsp. Parmesan cheese

Oil, to fry

For the soup:

1 onion, finely chopped

2 cloves garlic

3 tbsp. butter

20 oz / 260 g canned corn kernels

2 cups /500 ml low-fat milk

Salt & freshly milled pepper

7 oz /200 g American cheese, (processed cheese)

Scant ½ cup /100 g light (single) cream

2 beefsteak tomatoes

½ bunch fresh parsley, finely chopped

4 oz /100 g smoked salmon, to garnish

Method

Prep and cook time: 1 h

1 Bring the water to a boil and add ½ teaspoon of salt. Sprinkle the cornmeal slowly into the water, stirring continually to prevent clumping. Lower the heat, cover with a lid and cook for about 40–45 minutes, stirring from time to time. Add the butter and the Parmesan cheese and stir. Pour the polenta onto a cookie sheet to form a layer about ⅓ inch (1 cm) thick. Smooth evenly and let cool until firm.

2 For the soup, peel the onion and the garlic, cut in half, and then finely chop. Fry the onion and the garlic in butter. Drain the corn kernels and sauté ⅔ of the corn with the onions and garlic. Pour in the milk, bring to a boil, then purée and strain through a fine-mesh sieve. Season the soup with salt and pepper. Add the processed cheese and cream and simmer for about 10 minutes, stirring occasionally.

3 Place the tomatoes in hot water for a few seconds, then into cold water and peel. Cut the tomatoes into quarters, de-seed and chop. Wash the parsley, shake dry, and then finely chop. Cut the polenta into cubes and toast in a skillet until lightly browned.

4 Fry the chopped tomatoes together with the remaining corn kernels in butter until warm. Stir in the chopped parsley.

5 Break the salmon into pieces and season with pepper.

6 Pour the soup into 4 bowls. Add a few spoonfuls of the tomato-corn mix, followed by some diced polenta. Garnish with a few pieces of smoked salmon and serve hot. Serve the remaining polenta cubes on the side.

CARROT AND ORANGE SOUP

Ingredients

2 tbsp. butter

1 onion, chopped

6 carrots, peeled and grated

1 potato, baking, peeled and grated

2½ cups /600 ml vegetable broth (stock)

2 oranges, grated zest and juice

2 tbsp. crème fraîche

Dash Port wine

Pinch cayenne pepper

2 tbsp. fresh parsley, chopped

Salt & freshly milled pepper

Method

Prep and cook time: 30 min

1 Sauté the chopped onion in hot butter, add the grated carrots and potato, season with salt, cover and cook for about 5 minutes.

2 Now pour in enough vegetable broth (stock) so that the vegetables are covered. Add the orange zest, cover and simmer for a further 10 minutes.

3 Purée the soup until smooth. Add the orange juice and the crème fraîche and stir. Pour in a little vegetable stock, depending on the thickness of the soup.

4 Season to taste with Port wine, salt and cayenne pepper. Garnish with chopped parsley and freshly milled pepper and serve.

MINESTRONE WITH POTATO DUMPLINGS

Ingredients

9 oz /250 g carrots

3 stalks celery

I head of broccoli

2 tbsp. olive oil

2 sprigs rosemary

6 cups /1½ litre vegetable broth (stock)

⅓ cup /50 g frozen peas

3 tbsp. snipped chives

Salt & freshly milled pepper

3 tbsp. snipped chives

Grated Parmesan cheese

For the dumplings:

1 lb 12 oz /800 g baking potatoes

1 egg

3–4 tbsp. potato starch

3 tbsp. snipped chives

Method

Prep and cook time: 40 min

1 Wash, trim and thinly slice the carrots and celery. Cut the broccoli into florets.

2 For the dumplings, wash half of the potatoes and steam for about 30 minutes, until cooked. Peel and press through a potato ricer. Peel the rest of the potatoes, grate finely and add to the cooked potatoes. Stir in the egg and chives. Season with salt and add enough potato starch to produce a shapeable 'dough'. Cook a test dumpling in hot water. Then, with moistened hands form into about 20 small dumplings. Cook very gently in simmering, salted water for about 20 minutes.

3 Heat the oil in a pan and sauté the prepared vegetables (apart from the peas). Add the rosemary sprigs and the broth (stock), bring to a boil and simmer for about 15 minutes. Add the peas after 5 minutes. Season the soup to taste with salt and pepper. Put the drained dumplings and the rest of the chives into the soup, ladle into bowls and serve sprinkled with Parmesan cheese.

TOMATO AND BEET SOUP
WITH FETA CHEESE AND OREGANO

Ingredients

14 oz /400 g beet (beetroot)

3 cups /750 ml vegetable broth (stock)

7 oz / 200 g chopped tomatoes (canned)

Salt & freshly milled pepper

Juice of ½ lemon

4 oz / 100 g feta cheese, diced

Oregano, to garnish

Method

Prep and cook time: 30 min Chilling time: 2 h

1 Peel and dice the beet (beetroot) and simmer in the vegetable broth (stock) over a low heat for about 15 minutes.

2 Then add the tomatoes and simmer for a further 5 minutes. Blend in a blender.

3 Now either leave the soup to go cold and season to taste, or serve hot.

4 To serve hot, return to a boil, season with salt and pepper and add lemon juice to taste.

5 Put a little feta cheese in each bowl and ladle the soup over it (hot or cold). Serve garnished with oregano.

ANDALUSIAN FISH SOUP WITH CHILIES

Ingredients

1 lb 2 oz /500 g monkfish fillets, or sea bream, cleaned and cut into bite-size pieces

1 onion

2 cloves garlic

1 chili

1 sprig rosemary

4 tbsp. olive oil

4 tomatoes

2 yellow bell peppers

½ bunch basil

4 sprigs thyme

1¾ cups /400 ml tomato juice

¾–1 cup / 200 ml fish broth (stock)

Salt & freshly milled pepper

Tabasco sauce

Method

Prep and cook time: 25 min Marinating time: 2 h

1 Wash the fish fillets and pat dry. Cut into bite-size pieces. Peel the onion and the garlic, finely chop the garlic and roughly chop the onion. Wash the chili and cut into thin rings.

2 Finely chop the rosemary leaves. Mix with the oil, chili, garlic and fish and leave for about 2 hours to marinate.

3 Wash the tomatoes, halve and chop. Wash the bell peppers, halve, de-seed and chop. Finely chop the basil and thyme leaves. Save some of the leaves for the garnish.

4 Take the fish out of the marinade and fry in a skillet until golden brown, then remove. Heat the marinade in a large pan and sauté the onion. Add the bell pepper, the tomatoes and pour in the tomato juice and the fish broth (stock). Simmer gently for about 10 minutes. Mix in the chopped herbs and season to taste with salt, pepper and Tabasco sauce.

5 Place the fish in the soup and warm and serve.

TYROLEAN BARLEY SOUP WITH SMOKED PORK AND VEGETABLES

Ingredients

½ cup /100 g barley

1 onion

2 oz /50 g streaky bacon, diced

Salt & freshly milled pepper

Pinch nutmeg

3 cups /700 ml beef broth (stock)

7 oz /200 g smoked cured pork, without the bone, pre-cooked

8 oz / 250 g pumpkin

1 leek

2 stalks celery

A few celery leaves, to garnish

Method

Prep and cook time: 1 h

1 Wash the barley and drain well. Peel and finely chop the onion. Dice the bacon and fry in a skillet, without fat. Add the barley and the onions and sauté. Season with salt, pepper and nutmeg and pour in the beef broth (stock). Bring to a boil, and then simmer for 20–25 minutes.

2 In the meantime, cut the pork into -inch (2–3 cm) cubes. Dice the pumpkin, wash the leek and cut into thin rings, wash the celery and cut into slices. Put the pork and the vegetables in the soup and cook until soft.

3 Season the soup to taste, garnish with a few celery leaves and serve.

CAULIFLOWER CREAM WITH SCALLIONS

Ingredients

1 cauliflower

½ white onion

1 tbsp oil

Salt & ground white pepper

Pinch nutmeg

1 tsp. flour

2 cups /500 ml clear vegetable broth (stock)

Scant 1 cup /200 g light (single) cream

2–3 tbsp. lemon juice

4 small scallions (spring onions), including green tops

Method

Prep and cook time: 30 min

1 Wash the cauliflower and divide into florets. Cook in boiling, salted water until al dente. Drain the cauliflower. Refresh the cauliflower in cold water and drain well.

2 Peel and chop the onion. Fry in oil until soft. Put ¼ of the cauliflower florets on the side. Sauté the remaining cauliflower with the onions, then season with salt, pepper and nutmeg.

3 Sprinkle flour over the top and pour in the vegetable broth (stock). Simmer for about 10 minutes.

4 Pour in the cream and the lemon juice, purée until smooth and season to taste. Put the remaining cauliflower florets in the soup and warm.

5 Clean and trim the scallions (spring onion). Serve the soup in warmed bowls and garnish with a scallion.

WHITE BEAN AND CARROT SOUP

Ingredients

1¼ cups /250 g dried white beans

5 cups /1¼ litres cold water

1 large potato, boiling

1 fennel bulb, chopped

1 onion, chopped

4 cloves garlic, chopped

2 large carrots, chopped

1 tbsp. olive oil

2 tsp. chopped fresh sage leaves

1 tsp. chopped fresh rosemary leaves

Salt & freshly milled pepper

1 tbsp. grated Parmesan cheese

Handful fresh sage leaves, to garnish

Method

Prep and cook time: 1 h 30 min plus 12 hours soaking time

1 If using dried beans, put the beans in a bowl, cover with water and soak overnight.

2 Drain the beans, then pour in the cold water, bring to a boil, then simmer for about 1 hour.

3 Peel and chop the potato. Wash and trim the fennel bulb, cut in half lengthways and remove the core, then chop. Peel and finely chop the onion and the garlic. Peel and dice the carrot.

4 Fry the onions and the garlic in hot oil until soft. Add the potatoes, fennel and carrots and sauté. Then add to the beans and simmer for 20 minutes. Add the chopped sage leaves and rosemary leaves and season with salt and pepper.

5 Stir in the grated Parmesan cheese. Garnish with a few sage leaves and serve.

SPICY PEA AND VEGETABLE SOUP

Ingredients

²/₃ cup / 100 g brown dried peas

Olive oil

1 tsp. cumin seed

3 cloves garlic, finely chopped

4 scallions (spring onions), chopped

2 tsp. grated ginger

2 tsp. garam masala

2–3 green chillies, deseeded and finely chopped

14 oz/ 400 g cauliflower, divided into small florets

14 oz / 400 g pumpkin, diced

3 cups / 750 ml water

1 tsp. tomato puree

Salt

1–2 tbsp. sour cream, to garnish

Method

Prep and cook time: 1 h Soaking time: 12 h

1 Soak the peas in water overnight.

2 Drain and rinse the beans. Heat 4–5 tablespoons oil in a wide pan and briefly sauté the cumin seeds. Add the garlic, scallions (spring onions), ginger, garam masala and chili and sauté briefly.

3 Add the pumpkin and cauliflower, sauté briefly, then add the water. Stir in the tomato puree and peas, season with 1–2 teaspoons salt and bring to a boil. Then reduce the heat, cover and simmer over a low heat for 30–35 minutes.

4 Season to taste with salt. Ladle into soup bowls and serve. Add 1–2 tablespoons sour cream to each bowl, if desired.

RUSSIAN SOLYANKA WITH SOUR CREAM

Ingredients

9 oz /250 g potatoes

3 onions

2 red bell peppers

4 tbsp. butter

2 tbsp. tomato paste (purée)

6 cups /1½ litres broth (stock)

3 pickled gherkins

2 bay leaves

7 oz /200 g cooked beef

7 oz /200 g ring bologna sausage or mortadella sausage

7 oz /200 g smoked, cured pork, or other meat, cold roast, ham etc.

3 tbsp. small capers

Salt & freshly milled pepper

Paprika, noble sweet

Sugar

Good ¾ cup /200 g sour cream

Lemon slices

Dill weed (tips) to garnish

Method

Prep and cook time: 1 h

1 Peel and dice the potatoes. Peel and slice the onions. Deseed the peppers and cut into strips.

2 Heat the butter in a pan and sauté the onions and peppers until soft. Stir in the tomato paste (purée) and add the broth (stock).

3 Slice the gherkins into strips and add to the soup along with some of the gherkin liquid, bay leaves and potatoes. Simmer for at least 30 minutes or until soft.

4 Cut the sausage into strips. Dice the beef and smoked pork and add to the solyanka. Add the capers. Season with salt, pepper, paprika and sugar and stir in half the sour cream.

5 Ladle the solyanka onto plates and garnish each with 1 slice of lemon, a spoonful of cream and tips of dill weed.

PEA SOUP WITH CRÈME FRAÎCHE

Ingredients

1 shallot

1 clove garlic

1 tbsp. butter

$2^2/_3$ cups /400 g frozen peas

1 tsp. ginger, freshly grated

$2^1/_2$ cups /600 ml chicken broth (stock)

Scant ½ cup /100 ml whipping cream

Salt & freshly milled pepper

2 tbsp. crème fraîche

Method

Prep and cook time: 20 min

1 Peel and finely chop the shallot and garlic. Heat the butter and sauté the shallot and garlic, then add the peas and ginger. Stir in the chicken broth (stock) and bring to a boil.

2 Simmer the soup for 6–8 minutes, then add the cream and purée the soup finely. Push through a sieve if you wish.

3 Season to taste with salt and pepper and ladle into bowls. Add a swirl of crème fraîche to each and serve.

BUTTERNUT SQUASH SOUP

Ingredients

1 onion

1 clove garlic

1 tsp. ginger, finely grated

1 red chili

4 tbsp. oil

1 lb 12 oz /800 g butternut squash

1 tbsp. sugar

2 cups /500 ml vegetable broth (stock)

Scant ½ cup /100 ml orange juice

¾–1 cup / 200 g whipping cream

Salt & freshly milled pepper

1 tsp. curry powder

Ground nutmeg

Thyme, to garnish

For the croutons:

2 slices white bread, from the previous day

2 tbsp. butter

Method

Prep and cook time: 1 h

1 Peel and dice the onion and garlic. Wash the chili, slit open lengthways, remove the seeds and white inner ribs and chop finely. Peel and deseed and dice the butternut squash.

2 Heat the oil in a pan and sauté the butternut squash, onion, garlic, ginger and chili. Sprinkle with sugar and stir over the heat until lightly caramelized. Now add the broth (stock), cover and cook gently for about 35 minutes, until soft.

3 Purée the soup. Add the orange juice and cream and bring to a boil. Season with salt and pepper and add curry powder and nutmeg to taste.

4 To make the croutons, cut the white bread into cubes and fry in butter until golden brown. Season with salt and pepper and drain on a paper towel.

5 Ladle the hot soup into bowls and serve garnished with thyme and croutons.

CEP BROTH WITH MUSHROOM RAVIOLI

Ingredients

4 cups /1 litre chicken broth (stock)

2 tsp. cep powder

½ cup /125 ml dry white wine

1 leek, long, thin

350 g cep mushrooms, fresh, small

2 tbsp. butter

1 packet mushroom ravioli,
1 lb (500 g) packet or homemade

salt & freshly milled pepper

chervil leaves, to garnish

Homemade ravioli:

4 cups /400 g flour

4 eggs

1 tsp. olive oil

Salt

For the filling:

2 cups /200 g mushrooms, chopped

1 onion

1 tbsp. olive oil

9 oz /250 g Ricotta cheese

½ cup /50 g Pecorino cheese, grated

Salt & freshly milled pepper

Nutmeg

Method

Prep and cook time: 1 h Resting time: 30 min

1 Bring the chicken broth (stock), white wine and cep powder to a boil. Wash and clean the leek and cut into thin rings. Add to the broth, together with the ravioli. Bring to a boil, then simmer for a few minutes.

2 In the meantime clean the mushrooms, cut the ends off the stems and cut into slices. Heat the butter in a skillet and fry the cep mushrooms on both sides until golden brown. Season with salt and pepper.

3 Divide the cep mushrooms between 4 bowls, place a few raviolis on top and pour in a spoonful of broth. Garnish with chervil leaves and serve.

4 To make the homemade ravioli, mix the flour, eggs, oil and 1 teaspoon salt and knead to a smooth dough. Add a little water or flour if the dough is too dry or too wet. Form a ball, cover and leave to rest for about 30 minutes.

5 Clean the mushrooms and finely chop. Peel the onion and finely chop. Heat the olive oil in a skillet and fry the onions until soft. Add the mushrooms and sauté over a medium heat until all liquid has evaporated. Let cool. Mix in the ricotta and Pecorino cheese and season with salt, pepper and nutmeg.

6 Knead the dough. Use a pasta machine or roll out the dough thinly on a lightly floured surface. Place 1–2 teaspoons of mushroom mix on the dough. Leave about 1 ½ inches (3 cm) in-between. Cover with the second ravioli sheet and press the edges down well to seal. Use a pastry cutter to cut out the ravioli.

7 Cook the ravioli in boiling, salted water for 3–4 minutes.

VEGETABLE SOUP WITH BACON

Ingredients

2 leeks

1 carrot

14 oz /400 g baking potatoes

14 oz / 400 g celery root (celeriac)

8 slices bacon

3¼ cups /800 ml vegetable or chicken broth (stock)

1 sprig rosemary

Salt & freshly milled pepper

Ground nutmeg

2 tbsp. parsley, chopped

Method

Prep and cook time: 1 h

1 Wash and trim the leeks and cut into rings.

2 Peel the carrot, halve lengthways and slice.

3 Peel and dice the celery root (celeriac) and potatoes.

4 Fry the bacon in a dry pan (without adding any oil), then add the vegetables and broth (stock). Add the rosemary, cover and simmer for 20–30 minutes.

5 Season with salt and pepper and add nutmeg to taste. Finally, sprinkle with parsley and serve.

Published by Transatlantic Press

First published in 2010

Transatlantic Press
38 Copthorne Road, Croxley Green, Hertfordshire WD3 4AQ

© Transatlantic Press

Images and Recipes by StockFood © The Food Image Agency

Recipes selected by Aleksandra Malyska, StockFood

A catalogue record for this book is available from the British Library.

ISBN 978-1-907176-38-8

Printed in China